Mum put eggs in the pan.

Biff and Chip had a ping-pong set.

3

Mum put the eggs in egg cups.

Dad was in the shed.

Mum got fish and chips.

Chip was in his den.

Biff was on her bed.

Dad was back in the shed.

Mum was fed up.

Mum got a bell and a gong.

Mum had a hotpot.

She rang the bell.

Bang the gong, Kipper.

Dad ran in.
Biff and Chip ran in.